small batch
❱PRESERVING❰
made easy
·········· ········

Freezer and Fridge Jam, Jelly, Marmalade, Conserve, and Preserve Recipes

DISCLAIMER

Introduction

Small Batch Preserving Made Easy combines the brilliant flavor of essential fruits with the old-age act of preserving. Included are over twenty delicious recipes that provide loads of your favorite fruit-y flavors perfect for Holiday parties, on-the-run breakfasts and dessert toppings. In fact, each of the recipes reveals stunning flavor without the added store-bought preservatives; they are not pulsing with so much sugar that the jelly or jam forgets about its core fruit ingredient. This is beneficial not only for your waistline, but your overall health and your taste buds as well.

Preserving is not just for your grandmother anymore as you reap the frugal rewards of creating your personal jams and jellies, each ready in your fridge for up to a month and your freezer for up to a year. This book reveals intricate tips on the basics of preserving, leading you down this newfound path with confidence and a great thick-bottomed pot. Furthermore, this book breaks down the gelling process, bringing clarity to that most stressful part of any beginner's jam-making time. Your question, "Is it done yet?" will find its answer in the basics of preserving, and your jam will find its way safely into their cans or freezer-ready containers, without the unnecessary procedure of "canning".

Each jam, jelly, marmalade, preserve, and conserve in this book is unique and perfect for any gift-giving occasion. You're revealing a piece of your crafty self in each jam and jelly; you're bringing high-quality spreads to your breakfast table that retain nutritive qualities from their sunny fruit days. Allow your family and friends to taste the delicious, natural benefits of your at-home preserving abilities. Yield fruity, delicious flavor— without too much added sugar. Utilize high-quality ingredients, and administer natural sweetness in your life. Your dry toast and your taste buds are waiting.

Table of Contents

Chapter #1

BASICS OF PRESERVING

Preserving is not just your grandmother's game anymore. All your favorite seasonal summer produce can follow you into the winter with these stunning recipes, each with natural sweetness, with no preservatives, and ready for your English muffin morning spreading adventures, cheese plates, and booming Christmas parties.

When you create your own jam, you aren't signing on to the preservative-rich nature of other jams and jellies. The store-bought ones generally contain more sugar than anything nutritious. Furthermore, creating your own jam, jelly, or other preserves is actually the most frugal way in which to deliver high-quality spreads to your breakfast table.

With just some fruit, pectin, and some sugar, you can create this sweet treat to last an entire year.

Understanding the Gel State

When you begin creating your jams and jellies, you'll need to reach something called the "gel point." At this point, the created jam and jelly will, in fact, "gel" together when it cools to create a luxurious, beautiful spread. Many people utilize a candy thermometer; when the goop reaches 220 degrees Fahrenheit, the jelly should be done. However, there are other, more reliable ways in which to test the jam.

The Spoon or Sheet Test

Create this test by dipping a big spoon into the still-boiling jam. Lift the spoon, with the jam, a foot and a half into the air over the pot. Pour the jam out of the spoon quickly. Watch closely for the very last drop to fall off the spoon. During the initial stages of the jam-making process, the last drop will fall off in a single drop.

When the jelly begins to foam, it's close to being done. The bubbles should be spread over the surface, starting to rumble up the pot. During the last stages, the liquid-y jelly will fall off the spoon in two distinct drops—rather than the first step's one drop. However, when the jelly's completely ready, the drops will pour off the spoon and run into each other as they fall off. This means they "sheet" from the spoon.

The Wrinkle Test
Alternately, you can utilize the wrinkle test. Keep a plate in your freezer as you cook your jelly. When you feel that your jelly is ready—based on the spoon test—you can dot a very small amount of the jelly on the freezer plate. Place the freezer plate back in the freezer for a minute. Afterwards, if you press against the jelly with your finger and it wrinkles, it's ready to go.

The Pectin Perception
Most of the inspired recipes in this book utilize something called pectin. There are many reasons why. Essentially, when you cook your delicious fruits for

too long, the sweetness and brightness simply simmers away from them. Furthermore, the flavor becomes over-processed, and you don't end up with as much jam product as you should. Also, who wants to stand over a hot stove all day, stirring and sweating?

Pectin is natural. It is a fiber that lingers in the cell walls of fruits like apples and oranges. In fact, you can even make it at home, revealing the most natural product around! Simply boil two pounds of under-ripe green apples along with one tablespoon of lemon juice and about three and a half cups of water. Afterwards, strain the boiled mess through a cheesecloth. Then, continue to boil what you've strained to decrease the overall volume by fifty percent. This results in your natural pectin, perfect for your jam recipes. Many proponents of jam further state that experimenting with at-home pectin holds best results when mixing high-pectin fruits, like apples, with low-pectin fruits, like cherries.

Pectin allows your jam to reach its ideal texture. The jams and jellies can remain bright and spreadable. When you stick your knife into your prepared batch, you should create a luxurious experience. The color of the jam will be natural, bright red or sunny yellow, based on your desired fruity flavor.

Note: there are advantages to the use of commercial pectin. For one, the setting point on jams will be reached about ninety-nine percent of the time when cooking with commercial pectin. Many regular canners, however, do not advise commercial pectin because it requires the addition of too much extra sugar, which eventually reduces the overall fruity taste of the jam or jelly.

Fridge and Freezer Jams
The pros of these fridge and freezer jams versus their friendly relatives, the canned jams, are many. Essentially, when you create these fridge and freezer jams, you don't need to utilize as much sugar for preservation reasons. This means you're creating a naturally sweet, healthy option. Furthermore, you can utilize other types of sealable containers—not just jars—in order to

store the jams. This is because the jams and jellies are being preserved with the assistance of the refrigerator and freezer.

Chapter #2

TOOLS OF THE PRESERVING TRADE

To get started on you jamming adventure, you'll need:

1. A thick-bottomed pot. A jam-maker's favorite is an all-clad pot with a thick bottom. Look to the 8-ounce variety.
2. Various utensils, like knives, graters, food processors, mashers, measuring cups, and measuring spoons.
3. A mesh skimmer to slide off the foam from the rest of the product.
4. Jars.
5. Sterilizing equipment: a large, 12 quart stock pot, soap and water, 15 minutes of your time.

Tips to Sterilize Your Jars
It's incredibly important to sterilize your mason jars to escape future trouble with

mold—especially if you want these jams and jellies to last you a little while. You can either choose new jars or utilize old jars. Do not use mayo jars.

When you're beginning your sterilization process, choose from the right glass jars. Make sure none of them have cracks or inconsistencies. Furthermore, look to ones with a flat metal lid and round sealer. Many canners utilize Ball jars, found easily on the Internet.

Next, wash each jar, lid, and round sealer with soap and water. Completely rinse them out.

In your large, 12-quart stock pot, place each jar with its top up. Cover the jars with water, bringing the water two inches over the jars' heads. Allow the water to spring to a rolling boil on high heat for about fifteen minutes.

Afterwards, turn the stove off. Place the sealing lids and the round lids in the water, as well. Leave everything in the water for about twenty minutes. You can leave them in for just under an hour, if you like.

Remember to remove the jars with tongs, as the water might still be hot. When you remove them, place them on paper towel. When the jars are still warm, portion out your still-warm jams, jellies, or preserves in them. Note: when you administer hot ingredients into a room-temperature jar, the jar may crack. Afterwards, seal the lids.

Tips for Choosing Fresh Preserving Fruit

The best-quality fruits create the best-quality jellies and jams. Choose locally grown and organic whenever possible. Best-quality apples are ones with bright colors; look for raspberries and blueberries that are firm and oranges that are heavy. Generally speaking, the more robust a fruit, the riper it is.

Remember that under-ripe fruits contain a good deal more pectin than over-ripe fruits. Therefore, it's better to mix and match over-ripe apples, for example, with under-ripe apples. Furthermore,

15

fruits with high acid content, like crabapples, sour berries, grapes, and cranberries are perfect for the jam and jelly process. Always make sure to wash your fruit thoroughly before proceeding to make the jams and jellies.

# Chapter #3

JAM RECIPES

Jam is a delicious spread that is formulated by mixing fruit with sugar and pectin. Pectin, as you well know, is a soluble fiber found in the cell wall of many different fruits. When it's heated alongside water and sugar, it "gels" the other ingredients together. Jam is different from its other counterparts because it is a fruit spread that comes from crushed fruit or fruit pulp.

Sweet Summer Strawberry Jam

This strawberry jam is perfect for a quick jam fix in the summer months. Give the sweet treat to a friend or family member, or spread it over whole wheat bread for the perfect breakfast.

Prep Time: 20 minutes
Cook Time: 20 minutes
Makes: 5 cups

Ingredients:
4 cups sugar
¼ cup lemon juice

2 pounds hulled strawberries

Directions:

Begin by thoroughly washing the strawberries and crushing them together in a bowl. You should have about four cups of the mashed strawberries.

At the bottom of a thick-bottomed saucepan, pour together sugar, lemon juice, and the mashed berries. Stir this mixture over a low heat setting. The sugar will dissolve.

After the sugar dissolves, boost the stovetop heat to HIGH, and allow the mixture to come to a complete rolling boil. Continue to stir often until the jam reaches 215 degrees Fahrenheit.

Afterwards, remove the jam from the stovetop and transfer the mixture into clean jars. Remember to leave about a half-inch at the top of the jam jar. Place the seal on the jar, and refrigerate the jam immediately. Keep refrigerated for three weeks or place in the freezer for up to one year.

Kiki Kiwi and Strawberry Jam

This tropical sensation brings sweet, natural sensation to your taste buds.

Prep Time: 20 minutes
Cook Time: 20 minutes
Makes: 12 cups

Ingredients:
2 ½ cups chopped and peeled kiwi
1 tbsp. candied ginger
5 ½ cups strawberries
1 ¾ ounces powdered fruit pectin
4 ½ cups sugar

Directions:
Bring the strawberries into a large bowl, and mash them well. Add these mashed berries to a thick-bottomed saucepan, and add the ginger, lemon juice, and the kiwi. Pour in the pectin, and continue to stir. Place the stovetop heat on HIGH, and stir constantly as the mixture comes to a full boil.

Next, add the sugar. Allow the mixture to return to its rolling boil, and allow it to boil for one minute.

Afterwards, remove the jam from the heat, and swipe off the foam. Add the jam to your clean jars and allow them to retain a half inch of air on the top. Let the jam cool in their jars for one hour at room temperature. Then, cover the jars and allow them to continue to stand at room temperature for an additional twenty-four hours.

Afterwards, your jam is ready! Allow it to refrigerate for three weeks or freeze for twelve months. You can thaw your frozen jam in the refrigerator for about a day before serving.

Tropical Green Pineapple Jam

Delicious pineapple and kiwi jam is both sweet and sour; it's perfect on toasted bread, English muffins, or croissant.

Prep Time: 20 minutes
Cook Time: 15 minutes
Makes: 4 cups

Ingredients:
3 ¼ cups sugar
4 peeled and sliced kiwis
8 ounces mashed pineapples
3 ounces liquid fruit pectin
¼ cup lime juice

Directions:

In a big microwave-safe bowl, place the mashed pineapple, kiwi, sugar, and the lime juice. Stir well. Afterwards, microwave the mixture without a cover on HIGH for about ten minutes, or until it holds a full rolling boil. Make sure to remove the bowl every two minutes to give it a good stir. After ten minutes, add the liquid pectin and mix well.

Note: Make sure your microwave can retain 1,100 watts. If not, pour all the ingredients together in a thick-bottomed saucepan, and bring it to a boil on HIGH. After it's held a rolling boil for a full minute, add the liquid pectin.

Pour the jam into jars and allow the jam to cool at room temperature for two hours. Afterwards, cover the jam jars with their seals, and allow them to stand at room temperature for no longer than twenty-four hours. Refrigerate up to three weeks or freeze your jam for up to a year; enjoy when ready.

Greek Mediterranean Sun-Dried Tomato Jam

This savory, garlic-y jam sensation is the perfect substitute for your regular, average tomato paste.

Prep Time: 15 minutes.
Cook Time: 50 minutes.
Makes: 1 ½ cups.

Ingredients:
7 ounces sun-dried tomatoes in oil
1 minced garlic clove
1 diced onion
½ cup vegetable stock

1 cup water
1/3 cup red wine vinegar
1 tbsp. sugar
½ tsp. salt
1 tsp. basil
½ tsp. pepper

Directions:

Begin by draining the can of sun-dried tomatoes in oil and reserving one tablespoon of the oil to the side.

Prepare a thick-bottomed saucepan for the following steps.

Slice and dice the tomatoes and sauté the tomatoes and the diced onion in the reserved oil for about five minutes. Next, toss in the diced garlic, and cook for an additional minute.

Add the vegetable stock, water, sugar, vinegar, salt, basil, and pepper, and stir well. Allow the mixture to come to a boil. Afterwards, reduce the heat, cover the saucepan and allow the mixture to simmer for thirty minutes. Remove the cover, and allow the mixture to simmer for an additional twenty minutes. The liquid should completely evaporate.

Place the mixture in an airtight container, and refrigerate the jam for a week, eating on delicious pieces of garlic bread or alongside pasta.

Christmas Cranberry Jam

All the sweetness and cranberry goodness of a good holiday come together here in this Christmas Cranberry Jam, perfect for any family get together.

Prep Time: 5 minutes.
Cook Time: 20 minutes.
Makes: 14 cups.

Ingredients:
2 ½ quarts hulled strawberries or 40 ounces frozen strawberries
1 pound cranberries, fresh or frozen

27

6 ounces liquid fruit pectin
4 ½ pounds sugar

Directions:
Begin by bringing together the cranberries and the strawberries in the grinder or food processor. After you've mixed them together, place the mixture in a Dutch oven or thick-bottomed saucepan. Pour in the sugar, and stir well. Place the stovetop on HIGH, and bring the mixture to a rolling boil. Allow it to boil for one minute.

Afterwards, remove the mixture from the heat, and stir in the pectin. Return the mixture to the heat, and allow it to boil for an additional minute. Make sure to continuously stir.

Allow the mixture to cool for five or six minutes. Afterwards, slide off the foam, and portion out the jam into jars. Make sure to leave a half-inch at the top of each jar. Allow the jam to cool completely with the lids off for about an hour. Afterwards, place the lids on the jars and allow them to continue to cool in the refrigerator or the freezer. They can be refrigerated for three weeks or frozen for up to 12 months. Enjoy.

Chapter #4
JELLY RECIPES

Jelly, when compared to jam, holds quite a different consistently because it is formulated from the juice of fruits—not from the pulp. It is semi-solid, and is the result of sugar, pectin, and juice boiled together into a delicious element.

Papa's Pomegranate Jam

Pomegranate juice lends a most exquisite, interesting flavor atop any cracker or piece of cheese.

Prep Time: 15 minutes
Cook Time: 10 minutes
Makes: 6 cups

Ingredients:
1 ¾ ounces powdered fruit pectin
4 ½ cups sugar
4 cups pomegranate juice

Directions:

Begin by stirring together the pomegranate juice and the pectin in a thick-bottomed saucepan. Place the stovetop on HIGH and bring the mixture to a rolling boil. After it has boiled for one minute, add the sugar. Continue to stir, and allow it to boil once more for an additional two minutes.

Afterwards, remove the pan from the heat and slide off the foam. Pour the hot mixture into small jars and leave about a half-inch of space at the top of each jar. Allow the jelly to cool at room temperature with the lids off for one hour. Afterwards, place the lids on the jars and allow the jelly to sit out for a full twenty hours. Place the jelly in the refrigerator or in the freezer, afterwards, and enjoy the fridge jelly for three weeks or the freezer jelly for up to twelve months.

Farmer Bob's Blueberry Jelly

This recipe reveals a canning technique that completely seals the jars for ultimate storage. Plus, mounds and mounds of antioxidant-rich, delicious blueberries can be yours for essential English muffin-spreading!

Prep Time: 30 hours.
Cook Time: 1 hour 15 minutes.
Makes: 12 cups.

Ingredients:
4 cups water
6 ounces liquid fruit pectin

11 ½ cups sugar
2 quarts frozen or fresh blueberries

Directions:
Begin by placing the blueberries in a thick-bottomed saucepan, and crush them a little bit with the bottom of a cup. Next, add the water, and place the heat on the stovetop to high. Allow the mixture to boil, stirring occasionally. Afterwards, reduce the heat to medium, and cook without a cover for a full forty-five minutes.

Next, place three cheesecloth layers on a strainer. Place this strainer over a bowl, and pour the blueberry mixture over the strainer. Cover the blueberry mixture with the edges of the cheesecloth, and allow the strainer to strain for thirty minutes to yield six cups in the bowl below.

Pour this juice back into the thick-bottomed saucepan over high heat, and add in the sugar. Stir until the sugar begins to dissolve. Allow the mixture to boil, and add the pectin. Bring the mixture back to a boil, and allow it to boil for an additional minute.

Afterwards, remove the pot from the heat and remove the foam. Pour the mixture into small, clean jars, making sure to leave about a half-inch of space at the top of each mixture. Place the lids on the jars, and seal them tightly.

Store these jars in the refrigerator for up to three weeks or in the freezer for up to twelve months. You can thaw each of the jars for about twenty-four hours prior to serving. Enjoy.

Green Apple Green Pepper Jelly

This green pepper, green apple, and spicy jalapeno pepper mixture livens up any dry cracker at your next green event! Think: Earth Day, St. Patrick's Day, Green Sport Team Color Day, etc.

Prep Time: 10 minutes.
Cook Time: 20 minutes.
Makes: 5 cups.

Ingredients:
¾ cup diced green pepper
2 peeled and diced green apples
4 ½ cups sugar

1 ½ cups apple cider vinegar
¼ cup water
9 diced jalapeno peppers
6 ounces liquid fruit pectin
8 drops green food coloring (optional)

Directions:
Begin by bringing together apples, green peppers, jalapenos, sugar, apple cider vinegar, and water into a thick-bottomed saucepan. Bring this mixture to a boil on HIGH, stirring occasionally.

Next, reduce the heat and allow the mixture to simmer without a cover for ten minutes. Afterwards, strain this mixture and return what's left to the saucepan. Add the food coloring, and allow the mixture to come to a rolling boil as you stir consistently. Add the pectin, and allow it to boil for an additional minute.

Next, remove the mixture from the heat, and slide the foam from the top. Pour the hot mixture into small jars, leaving about a 1/2 inch of space between the jelly and the top of the jar. Place the lids on the jar, and screw them on tightly.

Allow the jelly to completely cool in the jars for about ten hours, and then place the jars in either the refrigerator or the freezer. You can refrigerator the jars for about three weeks, or you can freeze the jars for up to twelve months.

This jelly is perfect for gift-fiving or dressing up your next holiday party. Serve the jelly with delicious cream cheese and crackers for perfect party flavor.

Corn on the Cob Jelly

Sweet summertime corn comes to life in this jelly, a perfect slide away from your mainstay fruit jellies.

Prep Time: 10 Minutes.
Cook Time: 20 minutes.
Makes: 5 cups.

Ingredients:
10 corncobs
4 ½ cups water
2 ounces powdered fruit pectin
3 ¾ cup sugar
3 drops yellow food coloring

Directions:
Begin by slicing the corn kernels from their cobs. Place the corn to the side.

Place the corncobs in a thick-bottomed saucepan, and cover them with the water. Bring the ingredients to a boil on high, and allow them to boil for ten minutes, uncovered.

Next, toss out the cobs, and strain the rest of the liquid through a cheesecloth.

This should yield a liquid measurement of three cups.

Return the liquid to the saucepan, and add the pectin. Bring this mixture to a rolling boil. Afterwards, add the sugar, and bring it to a boil again. Immediately after it begins to boil, remove the foam, and add in the food coloring. Stir well.

Portion out the jelly into different jars, and cover them. You can refrigerate this jelly for two weeks or freeze it for one year. Enjoy.

Apple Cinnamon Jelly

Enjoy this stunning concoction to bring a spice of cinnamon into your life.

Prep Time: 5 minutes.
Cook Time: 20 minutes.
Makes: 7 cups.

Ingredients:
1 quart of apple juice
2 ounces powdered fruit pectin
5 drops red food coloring
3 tbsp. lemon juice
1 tsp. cinnamon
5 cups sugar

Directions:

Begin by bringing together the pectin, apple juice, lemon juice, and red food coloring in a thick-bottomed saucepan. Allow the mixture to come to a complete rolling boil. Make sure to continue stirring. Afterwards, add the sugar, and allow the mixture to return to boiling. Boil for an additional two minutes.

Afterwards, remove the foam from the jelly. Toss in the cinnamon, and stir. Portion out the jelly into small jars, making sure to leave about a half-inch of space between the jelly and the jar tops. Allow the jelly to cool at room temperature for about ten hours. Afterwards, refrigerate the jelly for up to three weeks or freeze the jelly for up to a year.

Chapter #5
MARMALADE RECIPES

Marmalade is essentially a form of jam; however, it is generally made with citrus fruits such as oranges, lemons, and limes. A few other marmalades have snuck in through the cracks over the years, creating a diverse group of spreads. Find raspberry, ginger, and rhubarb alongside the citrus mainstays.

Raging Raspberry Marmalade

Raspberry, your seedy friend, is ready with rich, sweet flavor. Pair the raspberry marmalade with whole grain toast for a delightful start to your day.

Prep Time: 20 minutes.
Cook Time: 0 minutes.
Makes: 8 cups.

Ingredients:
11 cups raspberries
2 ½ cups sugar
3 ounces liquid fruit pectin
1 cup corn syrup

3 tbsp. lemon juice

Directions:
Begin by completely crushing the raspberries one cup at a time to yield exactly three cups of crushed raspberries. Place these three cups in a large bowl. Afterwards, pour in the sugar and the corn syrup. Stir well, and allow this mixture to stand for ten minutes.

Next, add the lemon juice and the liquid pectin. Continue to stir for three minutes for perfect distribution. Next, add the other raspberries—the ones you didn't smash to yield three cups. These are whole raspberries.

Next, fill your jars with this mixture, and cover the jars with their lids. Allow the marmalade to stand for twenty-four hours at room temperature. Place the jars in the refrigerator for three weeks, or allow them to freeze for up to twelve months.

Simple Southern Orange Marmalade

Orange marmalade is perhaps the most well-known spread in the world. It's an essential part of your spreading routine; spread it on your favorite biscuit or piece of cheese today.

Prep Time: 15 minutes + 12 hours between cooks.
Cook Time: 2 hours and 45 minutes
Makes: 8 cups.

Ingredients:
4 seedless oranges

2 ½ lemons
7 ½ cups sugar

Directions:
Begin by slicing both the oranges and
the lemons in half. Proceed down the
sides of the fruits to create half-moon
pieces. Remove all seeds, and place
each piece into a large, thick-bottomed
pot. Pour in 8 cups of water, and allow
the mixture to boil. Make sure to stir
often. After it begins to boil, remove the
mixture and add in all the sugar. The
sugar will dissolve. Next, cover the
mixture and allow it to stand for 12
hours.

After twelve hours, bring the mixture
back to a boil. After it reaches its boiling
point, place the heat on low and allow it
to simmer without a cover for two hours.
After two hours, place the heat on
medium and continue to boil gently. Stir
occasionally. After thirty minutes,
remove any prepared foam.

Afterwards, portion the marmalade out
into sterilized jars. Place the lids on

each of the jars, and store them in the refrigerator for up to a year.

Lemon Lime Marmalade

Your ticket to morning sweet and sour flavor comes prepared in this lemon lime marmalade.

Prep Time: 10 minutes plus 12 hours standing time before cooking.
Cook Time: 2 hours.
Makes: 4 cups.

Ingredients:
8 limes
3 lemons
3 pounds granulated sugar
6 cups water

Directions:

Begin by juicing all the fruits, and bringing the juice into a large pan filled with six cups of water. Add the membranes and pulps to the pan, as well. Next, slice up the exterior peels of each lime and lemon, and place the peels inside the pan with the water, the membranes, and the juices. Allow this mixture to soak together for 12 hours.

After twelve hours, place this pot on the stovetop and turn the heat to high. Bring it to a boil. Afterwards, turn the heat to low and allow it to simmer for two hours.

Next, pour in the sugar and allow it to dissolve in the mixture. Bring the mixture to a rolling boil. When it seems set and more solid than liquid, remove the pan from the heat. Allow the mixture to cool for a full ten minutes.

Afterwards, portion out the tangy marmalade into jars. Seal all the jars tightly, and store them in the refrigerator for up to a year.

Ruby Rhubarb Marmalade

Super-sour on its own, rhubarb creates a wonderful taste when paired with sugar and oranges in this marmalade recipe. Remember that rhubarb leaves are completely toxic—just eat the stems!

Prep Time: 15 minutes.
Cook Time: 1 ½ hours.
Makes: 8 cups.

Ingredients:
6 cups frozen or fresh chopped rhubarb
5 ½ cups sugar
3 oranges

Directions:

Bring together the sugar and the rhubarb in a thick-bottomed pot. To the side, place the oranges—including their peels—in a food processor. Grind them up, and add them to the pot. Stir well, and bring the mixture to a boil. When it begins to boil, reduce the heat to low and allow it to simmer for one hour.

Afterwards, remove the mixture from the heat. Slice off the foam, and portion the marmalade into the jars. Make sure to leave about a half-inch of space between the top of the marmalade and the top of the jar.

Allow the marmalade to cool for two hours, and then place the lids on the jars. The marmalade keeps well in the refrigerator for up to twelve months.

Morning Glory Ginger Marmalade

Ginger is pulsing with essential nutrients and medicinal benefits. And it's delicious over bread, croissant, English muffin, and licked off a knife!

Prep Time: 15 minutes.
Cook Time: 1 hour and 40 minutes.
Makes: 5 cups.

Ingredients:
3 cups peeled and diced ginger
5 cups sugar
4 cups water

3 ounces liquid pectin

Directions:

Begin by dicing up the ginger to create three cups of it. Bring the ginger and the water together in a large pan. Heat the mixture over medium, and bring it to a boil. Afterwards, place the heat on low and allow the mixture to simmer. Place the lid on the pot, and let it to continue to simmer for one hour and fifteen minutes.

Next, pour the pan contents through a strainer and keep a half-cup of the ginger water. Place the cooked ginger in with the retained water, and allow it to sit together in the refrigerator for at least four hours.

After the ginger and water is completely cooled, place the mixture in a thick-bottomed pan. Add the sugar, and allow the mixture to come to a boil. Boil for one minute, consistently stirring. After one minute, add the pectin, and place the heat on low. Allow the mixture to simmer, stirring occasionally, for seven minutes.

Afterwards, skim the foam from the top of the marmalade, and portion the marmalade into each of the jars. Make sure to leave a half-inch space between the top of the marmalade and the top of the jar. Allow the marmalade to sit at room temperature for a full hour prior to placing the lid on the jars. The jars will keep in the refrigerator for up to a year. Enjoy!

Chapter #6
PRESERVE RECIPES

A preserve is formulated much like jams, jellies, and marmalades; however, it utilizes solid forms of fruits—and, occasionally, vegetables—alongside sugar and pectin to formulate a delicious spread.

Almond Cherry Pie Preserves

The consistency of this cherry pie almond preserve is like that of cherry pie: it's perfect for topping on fresh bread, pancakes, toast, and ice cream.

Prep Time: 5 minutes.
Cook Time: 25 minutes.
Makes: 11 cups.

Ingredients:
4 pounds pitted sour cherries
9 cups sugar
1 ½ cups water
6 ounces liquid fruit pectin

1 tsp. almond extract

Directions:

Begin by bringing together the pitted sour cherries and the water in a thick-bottomed saucepan. Stir them together, and boil the mixture for about fifteen minutes.

Afterwards, add the sugar. Bring this mixture to a complete rolling boil on high heat. Make sure to continue stirring constantly. Allow it to boil for four minutes, and then add your pectin. Boil for an additional minute prior to removing from heat.

Next, remove the mixture from the heat, and slide off the foam. Add the almond extract, and give it one or two good stirs. Portion the steamy mixture into jars, and leave about a half inch top between the preserves and the top of the lid. Place the lids on the jars, screwing them on tightly.

Next, allow each of the preserve jars to cool for about ten hours at room temperature. Place the jars in the refrigerator for up to three weeks, or allow them to freeze for up to a year. Enjoy the wonderful goodness of your cheery preserves!

Georgia Peach Preserves

Prep Time: 10 minutes.
Cook Time: 35 minutes.
Makes: 8 cups.

Ingredients:
12 pitted and chopped peaches
2 ounces powdered fruit pectin
4 cups sugar

Directions:
Begin by crushing the peaches one cup at a time in order to reveal one full cup of crushed peaches. Pour these peaches in the bottom of a thick-

bottomed saucepan. Add the rest of the uncrushed diced peaches overtop. Place the pot on medium-low heat, and allow it to boil for about twenty minutes. The peaches should become almond liquid.

Next, add the prepared peaches to a large bowl. Take out six cups of these peaches, and pour them back into the saucepan. Add the sugar to the saucepan, and allow this mixture to boil, stirring often, over medium heat. After it begins to boil, add the pectin. Boil for an additional minute.

After one minute, remove the pot from the heat, and portion the preserves into jars. Place each of the jars in either the refrigerator for up to a month or in the freezer for up to a year. Enjoy the Georgia goodness of each peach preserve!

Citrus Eggplant Preserves

Southeast Europe reveals its perfect eggplant preserve recipe, which is great over toasted bread or crackers. This savory sweet reveals nothing of the past bitterness of the vegetable.

Prep Time: 2 hours.
Cook Time: 15 minutes.
Makes: 8 cups.

Ingredients:
2 ½ pounds peeled and cubed eggplants
4 cups sugar

zest from 1 lemon
¼ cup lemon juice
2 tbsp. sesame seeds
1 tsp. grated ginger
2 tbsp. honey

Directions:
Begin by boiling water in a large pot. Place the cubes of eggplant into the water for three minutes. Afterwards, drain the pot through a strainer, and press each of the eggplant cubes to remove their liquid.

Next, place the eggplant cubes in a large pan with the sugar. Stir the mixture, and allow it to sit out for two hours. Try to stir it once every half hour. The sugar should dissolve into the mixture.

Afterwards, add the lemon juice, the lemon zest, and the ginger. Bring this mixture over medium heat on the stovetop. Stir it slowly for about fifteen minutes.

Add the honey and the sesame seeds, and remove the mixture from the heat.

Pour the preserves into small jars, and allow the preserves to cool for about two hours. Afterwards, place the lids on the preserves, and place them in either the refrigerator or the freezer. They keep well in the refrigerator for about a month, and they keep in the freezer for up to a year.

Vanilla Bean Plum Preserves

Prep Time: 10 minutes.
Cook Time: 55 minutes
Makes: 4 cups.

Ingredients:
1 ½ pounds diced plums
2 cups white sugar
4 cinnamon sticks
2 halved vanilla beans
juice from 1 lemon
1 ½ pounds diced apricots

Directions:

Begin by placing the sugar, plums, vanilla beans, and cinnamon sticks in a thick-bottomed, large pan. Squeeze all of the lemon juice into the mixture, and stir well. Bring the stovetop to medium-high heat beneath the mixture, and allow it to cook until boiling. This will take about ten minutes.

Next, switch the heat to medium, and stir occasionally, allowing it to simmer for about forty minutes. When it begins to set, place the stovetop on medium-high once more. Bring the mixture to a boil, and then add the apricots. Place the heat back to medium, and allow the mixture to simmer for about five minutes. Now, remove the cinnamon sticks.

Portion the preserves into your jars, making sure to leave a half-inch of space between the top of the preserves and the top of the jar. Allow the preserves to solidify at room temperature for one hour. Next, place the lids on the jars, and place them in the refrigerator or the freezer. They keep

in the freezer for a full year and in the
refrigerator for a month. Enjoy!

Chapter #7
CONSERVE RECIPES

Conserves are more complex cousins to the jam family. Conserves are usually made up of two fruits or more, and usually utilize nuts or dried fruits.

Sunny Fig and Pistachio Conserve

Prep Time: 10 minutes.
Cook Time: 25 minutes.
Makes: 3 cups.

Ingredients:
1 ¼ pounds diced figs
2 cups sugar
½ cup orange juice
zest from 2 oranges
½ tsp. cinnamon
2 tbsp. lemon juice
¼ tsp. cloves
½ cup shelled pistachios

72

Directions:

Begin by combining diced figs, sugar, orange zest, orange juice, lemon juice, cloves, and cinnamon together in a thick-bottomed saucepan. Bring the ingredients to a boil, stirring well in order to completely dissolve the sugar. Allow the mixture to boil on a medium-high heat for about ten minutes. Afterwards, add the pistachios.

Next, portion out the mixture into jars, making sure to leave a half-inch between the conserve and the top of the jar. Place the lids on the jars, and allow the conserve to cool for twenty-four hours at room temperature. Afterwards, place the conserve in either the refrigerator for three weeks or the freezer for up to a year.

Plum and Raisin Conserve

Golden raisins, oranges, and lemons come together to formulate this delicious conserve.

Prep Time: 10 minutes.
Cook Time: 50 minutes.
Makes: 7 cups.

Ingredients:
3 ½ pounds ripe plums
zest from 1 orange
juice from 1 orange
zest from 1 lemon
juice from 1 lemon
4 cups sugar
1 ¼ cup golden raisins
1 cup diced walnuts
1 tsp. cinnamon

Directions:
Begin by pitting and slicing the plums. Place the plums in a food processor or grinder, and pulse them about four times. They should be chopped.

Afterwards, place the prepared plums in a thick-bottomed saucepan or pot. Add the orange zest, orange juice, sugar, lemon zest, lemon juice, cinnamon, and the raisins. Bring the ingredients to a boil on high heat and stir consistently until the mixture is thick. This should take about forty-five minutes. Add the walnuts and stir.

Next, portion out the conserve into your jars with about a half-inch of space between the conserve and the top of the jar. Allow the conserve to cool with the lids off for one hour. Afterwards, place the lids on the jars and allow the conserves to continue to sit at room temperature for one day.

Place the jars in the refrigerator for up to three weeks or in the freezer for up to a year. Enjoy your delicious, irresistible raisin and walnut-filled plum conserve.

Christmas Ginger Pear Conserve

This conserve mixes the stunning sweetness of cranberries with pear and ginger flavor; it's essential for any Christmas party cheese plate.

Prep Time: 1 hour.
Makes: 4 cups.

Ingredients:
1 sliced orange
6 cups diced pears
2 cups sugar
1 cup frozen or fresh cranberries
1 lemon
2-ich diced strip of ginger

Directions:
Begin by chopping the pears and slicing the orange into very thin slices. After you've sliced the orange, dice it into very small pieces.

In a large, thick-bottomed pot, bring together the cranberries, orange, pears, and the sugar. Allow this mixture to simmer on low. Stir occasionally.

To the side, zest and juice the lemon. Dice up the ginger, as well. Pour the lemon juice, the lemon zest, and the ginger into the thick-bottomed pot, and stir well.

Next, boost up the heat to high, and allow the mixture to boil. Cook the mixture for about forty minutes. The fruit will be very soft, and the syrup will be nearly clear.

Afterwards, remove the mixture from the heat, and portion out the mixture into jars. Cover the jars, and refrigerate them for up to four weeks. Alternately, you can freeze the jars for up to one year. Simply thaw the frozen jars in the refrigerator approximately one day prior to your Christmas party!

Maple Syrup Blueberry Conserve

Prep Time: 1 ½ hours.
Makes: 5 cups.

Ingredients:

2 ½ cups frozen or fresh blueberries
2/3 cup maple syrup
½ cup water
1 tbsp. lemon juice
½ cup dried currants
1 ¼ cup dark brown sugar
½ cup diced pecans
½ tsp. cinnamon

Directions:

Begin by placing the blueberries in a food processor and chopping them. Place the processed blueberries in a thick-bottomed saucepan, and add lemon juice, maple syrup, and water. Bring this mixture to a boil on high heat, stir occasionally. After it begins to boil, place the heat on low, and allow it to simmer for five minutes.

Next, add the currants and the brown sugar. Return the mixture to a simmer and allow it to simmer, stirring occasionally, for thirty minutes. The mixture will thicken. After thirty minutes, remove the mixture from the heat, and add the cinnamon and the pecans.

Afterwards, portion the conserve into the jars, making sure to leave about a half-inch of space at the top of the jar. Allow the conserve to cool in the jar, with the lids off, for a full two hours. Afterwards, place the conserve in the refrigerator or the freezer. The jars will keep in the fridge for a full two months; they'll keep in the freezer for about a year. Enjoy.

Conclusion

Small Batch Preserving Made Easy: Fridge and Freezer Jam, Jelly, Marmalade, Conserve, and Preserve Recipes brings home preserving to your kitchen in several simplistic steps. It holds your hand as you work through your first days of jar sterilization, of the gelling process, and that never-before-understood ingredient: pectin. It fuels you to create stunning, deliciously intricate jellies, jams, preserves, marmalades, and conserves without the preservative-rich nonsense of the store-bought products. Whatever your fancy: strawberries, blueberries, figs, or corn on the cob, this recipe book brightens your sweet tooth, your holiday party, and your morning ritual. It rectifies many a piece of toast and many a croissant; it further amps up your cheese plates and desserts. Go ahead: fill up your freezer with as many recipes as you can make. Your taste buds will thank you!

Printed in Great Britain
by Amazon.co.uk, Ltd.,
Marston Gate.